Cooking with Napalm

Ernie S. Irwin

with photography by Christopher J. Watson

---

www.cookwithnapalm.com

Copyright 2011, Ernie S. Irwin

Introduction

Cooking With Napalm first started after I had decided to purchase several Bhut Jolokia (Ghost Chili) plants. After the harvest, I ended up with more peppers than I knew what to do with.

Of course, the very first thing I did was dice up one of the peppers and pop it in my mouth. Initially, I was slightly disappointed... I expected my face to melt immediately. But then, I began to taste the *amazing flavors* of the pepper -- unlike any other I've ever tasted!

It was fruity, earthy, sweet and pungent. It was delicious! Then, just like that, the heat began to intensify over and over again. It went from bearable to downright hallucinogenic.

The fire spread into my ears, down my throat and into my stomach. This was exactly what I was looking for! I had gotten more than I bargained for: a ridiculously spicy pepper that not only had the heat but also had the most distinguished and fantastic flavors.

Since I love to cook, I was excited to try and find recipes that used the Ghost Chili. But... I was dismayed when my search turned up nothing but a few predictable, boring dishes. In fact, most people claimed that the Ghost Chili was nothing more than a novelty!

I made it my mission to create the first collection of dishes that showcased the Ghost Chili (as well as other extremely hot varieties) and did more than just exploit them for their heat. I wanted to answer my own question... how do you cook with napalm?

This book, and the 48 beautifully photographed, delicious recipes inside is the answer to that question. Cooking With Napalm proves that wildly spicy food can be flavorful and complex without being overwhelming.

This is your guide to creating delicious food using the hottest peppers on the planet. Remember, it is a guide, so feel free to experiment and adjust the heat levels to your liking.

You don't have to love spicy food, you just have to love food.

The Food

Ghost Oil	Page 4
Assault and Pepper	Page 6
Harakiri Sauce	Page 8
Ghost Chili Salsa	Page 10
Assassination Wings	Page 12
NY Strip Steak and Whiskey Diablo Sauce	Page 14
Haitian Sunset Cocktail	Page 16
Eggs Benedict	Page 18
Ghostpacho	Page 20
Sriracha Sauce	Page 22
Truly Deviled Eggs	Page 24
For Whom The Bell Tolls	Page 26
Ghost Chili Truffles	Page 28
Bruchetta	Page 30
Mango Habanero Wings	Page 32
Ghost Vodka Sauce and Penne with Prosciutto	Page 34
Seared Salmon with Thai Sauce	Page 36
Fool's Gold Sauce	Page 38
Bahn Mi with Pickled Carrots and Daikon	Page 40
These Fries Aren't From France	Page 42
Sausage and Swiss Chard Pasta	Page 44
Shrimp and Scallop Ceviche	Page 46
Chicken Panang Curry	Page 48
Grilled Caribbean Flank Steak with Mo'Jolokia Sauce	Page 50
Trio of Chili Sorbets	Page 52
Clams Casino	Page 54
Cuban Missile Crisis Burgers with Ghost Chili Relish	Page 56
Thai Fried Rice	Page 58
Ghost Chili Bolognese	Page 60
Pineapple Ravioli with Devil's Tongue	Page 62
Straight Razor Cocktail	Page 64
Scalloped Potatoes	Page 66
Mussels and Chorizo	Page 68
Thai Hot Wings	Page 70
Fettuccine with Bacon, Goat Cheese and Roasted Asparagus	Page 72
Chicken Tikka Masala	Page 74
Steak Die-Anne	Page 76
Coconut Milk and Mango Panna Cotta	Page 78
Ghost Chili Pizza	Page 80
Stuffed French Toast with Spicy Syrup	Page 82
Voodoo Chili	Page 84
Curried Sea Scallops & Risotto au Terre	Page 86
Habanero Pork Tenderloin with Apple Lambic Glaze	Page 88
Russian Roulette Poppers	Page 90
Phaal	Page 92
Sesame Chicken	Page 94
Chocolate Pot de Creme	Page 96
Mango Lassi	Page 98

Ghost Oil
Ghost chili infused vegetable oil

Method

Slice the GHOST CHILIES in half and push down into the VEGETABLE OIL. Tightly seal the cap.

Allow the GHOST OIL to sit in a dry, dark place (pantry) for at least a week. The longer the chili and the oil sits, the more intense the heat is going to become.

Every few days, check on it and give it a good shake to mix up the particles.

Yield: Makes 28 ounces.

Ingredient List

(28 oz) **Vegetable Oil**
(2) **Ghost Chili**

Although incredibly simple to execute, having this napalm staple on hand is essential to infusing your cuisine with the heat and flavor of the Ghost Chili Pepper.

Use for deep frying, stir-frying and in any recipe that calls for cooking oil.

Assault and Pepper

A fiery gourmet finishing salt and pepper brimming with smoky flavor

Preparation

De-stem WHITE and CHOCOLATE HABANEROS. Using a mortar and pestle, grind the WHITE HABANEROS into a salt like consistency and set aside.

In the mortar and pestle, grind the CHOCOLATE HABANEROS into a "Crushed Red Pepper Flake" consistency.

Method

In a small bowl, mix KOSHER SALT and WHITE HABANERO. In another small bowl, mix BLACK PEPPER and CHOCOLATE HABANERO.

Store separately for up to 6 months.

Yield: Makes 1 cup each of salt and pepper.

Ingredient List

- (3) **Dried White Habanero**
- (3) **Dried Chocolate Habanero**
- (1 cup) **Kosher Salt**
- (1 cup) **Black Pepper**

This can be used in any dish that calls for salt and pepper and is a great way to quickly add smoky flavor and tons of heat to a dish.

Harakiri Sauce

A ghost chili hot sauce that balances extreme heat with fantastic flavors

Method

In a large pot over medium heat, combine the GARLIC, CARROTS, VINEGAR and SUGAR.
Simmer for 5 minutes.

Add ORANGES, TOMATO, GHOST CHILI and CHOCOLATE HABANERO.

Season with SALT and WHITE PEPPER.

Simmer for 25 minutes.
Remove from the pot in small batches and place in a blender.
Blend until smooth (about 5 minutes per batch).

This sauce can be used in place of fresh Ghost Chili Peppers in most of the savory recipes in this book.

4 tbsp of Harakiri Sauce is the equivalent of 1 Ghost Chili.

Yield: Makes 48 ounces.

Ingredient List

(6 cloves, minced) Garlic
(4, diced) Carrots
(1/2 cup) Vinegar
(1/4th cup) Sugar
(4, peeled and diced) Oranges
(3, diced) Tomatoes
(7, minced) Ghost Chili
(4, minced) Chocolate Habanero
(1 tbsp) Kosher Salt
(1 tbsp) White Pepper

This sauce is so ridiculously hot that I would caution you to use small amounts.

Its balance of sweet, salty, earthy and tangy flavors with atomic heat makes it hard to stop eating – but eat too much and you might feel like you just committed Harakiri with a spoon...

Ghost Chili Salsa
Fresh tomato salsa laced with lime juice and ghost chili

Method

Mix TOMATO, CILANTRO, ONION, GHOST CHILI, GARLIC, LIME JUICE and CUMIN together in a glass bowl.

Season with SEA SALT and BLACK PEPPER. Set aside in refrigerator to chill until serving.

Serve with tortilla chips.

Yield: Serves 5.

Ingredient List

(5, diced) **Tomato**
(4 tbsp. chopped) **Cilantro**
(2 tbsp. diced) **Onion**
(1 tbsp, minced) **Ghost Chili**
(3 cloves, minced) **Garlic**
(3 tbsp) **Lime Juice**
(1/2 tsp) **Cumin**
(1 tsp) **Sea Salt**
(1/2 tsp) **Black Pepper**

This tomato and ghost chili salsa is a great way to introduce the power and unique flavor of the chili to someone who has never had it before.

Assassination Wings

A deceiving wing coated in a murderous spice dust and fried in ghost oil

Preparation

In large container, combine BUTTERMILK and 2 tbsp GHOST CHILI SAUCE. Add CHICKEN WINGS and marinate overnight.

Fill deep fryer with GHOST OIL and preheat to 375 degrees.

In small container combine FLOUR, PAPRIKA, CAYENNE PEPPER, OREGANO, BASIL, THYME, ROSEMARY, DRIED CHOCOLATE HABANERO, DRIED WHITE HABANERO, SALT, BLACK PEPPER, and DRIED GHOST CHILI.

In another small container, create egg wash by whisking together EGGS, WATER and 2 tbsp GHOST CHILI SAUCE.

Method

Remove CHICKEN WINGS from marinade and dip into EGG WASH. Roll wing into the FLOUR AND SPICE MIXTURE to completely cover. Repeat the EGG WASH and FLOUR step.

Drop wings into deep fryer and fry until crispy and golden brown, about 12 minutes. Serve with ranch dipping sauce.

Yield: Makes 12 Assassination Wings.

Ingredient List

- (2 cups) Buttermilk
- (4 tbsp) Ghost Chili Sauce
- (12) Chicken Wings
- (for frying) Ghost Oil
- (2 cups) Flour
- (2 tsp) Paprika
- (1 tbsp) Cayenne Pepper
- (1/2 tsp) Oregano
- (1 tbsp, minced) Basil
- (1 tbsp minced) Thyme
- (1 tbsp minced) Rosemary
- (3, crushed) Dried Choc. Habanero
- (3, crushed) Dried White Habanero
- (1 1/2 tsp) Kosher Salt
- (2 tsp) Black Pepper
- (3, crushed) Dried Ghost Chili
- (2) Eggs
- (2 oz) Water

You don't realize the danger of these wings until it is too late. Your friends will never see it coming.

NY Strip Steak and Whiskey Diablo Sauce
Grilled strip steaks topped with a hellishly delicious sweet and tangy sauce

Preparation
Preheat oven to 325 degrees.
Cut ½ inch off of top of GARLIC bulb, remove papery skin and place on aluminum foil. Drizzle GHOST OIL over the GARLIC and cover. Bake in preheated oven for 1 hour.

Method
In medium saucepan over medium-high heat, combine WATER, PINEAPPLE JUICE, TERIYAKI SAUCE, SOY SAUCE, BROWN SUGAR and DEVILS TONGUE.
Heat the mixture to a boil and lower to a gentle simmer.
Add WHISKEY, PINEAPPLE CHUNKS, LEMON JUICE, ONION and BLACK PEPPER. Squeeze the roasted GARLIC until it turns into a paste. Whisk PASTE into the sauce and simmer for 30 minutes. Adjust seasoning to taste with SALT.

Season both sides of the NEW YORK STRIP STEAKS with SALT and PEPPER. Turn grill to high heat and add STEAKS.
Cook until desired doneness, flipping once halfway through Allow STEAKS to rest several minutes.
Serve steaks and top with the WHISKEY DIABLO SAUCE.

Yield: Serves 4.

Ingredient List
- (1 bulb) Garlic
- (1 tbsp) Ghost Oil [or Olive Oil]
- (2/3rd cup) Water
- (1 cup) Pineapple Juice
- (1/4th cup) Teriyaki Sauce
- (1 tbsp) Soy Sauce
- (1 1/3rd cup) Dark Brown Sugar
- (2 tbsp, minced) Devil's Tongue
- (2 tbsp) Whiskey
- (1 tbsp) Pineapple Chunks
- (3 tbsp) Lemon Juice
- (3 tbsp) White Onion
- (1 tbsp) Black Pepper
- (1 tbsp) Kosher Salt
- (4) New York Strip Steaks

Coat anything with the Whiskey Diablo Sauce to make it incredibly tasty.

It even makes less than favorite vegetables worth eating!

Haitian Sunset Cocktail
Vodka mixed with mint and fruit juices, topped with a shot of dark rum

Method

Hollow out CLEMENTINE.

In an ice filled shaker, combine VODKA, ORANGE JUICE and PINEAPPLE JUICE.

Shake vigorously and strain into large cocktail glass, over ice.

Place MINT in palm of your hand and smack to release aromatics.

Garnish with MINT and CHOCOLATE HABANERO.

Fill Clementine with DARK RUM.
Carefully float the CLEMENTINE in the cocktail.

Yield: Makes 1 Haitian Sunset.

Ingredient List
- (1) Clementine
- (1 oz) Vodka
- (2 oz) Orange Juice
- (4 oz) Pineapple Juice
- (garnish) Mint
- (1) Chocolate Habanero
- (1 oz) Dark Rum

This cocktail was inspired by a strikingly beautiful picture of a sunset in Haiti several days after the 2010 earthquake.

Pushing the clementine into the glass will spill the dark rum into the drink, causing a "sunset", leaving only the habanero "moon" floating.

Eggs Benedict
Poached eggs with canadian bacon served with a scorching hollandaise sauce

Method

In a small pan over low heat add 2 sticks of BUTTER and allow to melt. Skim milk solids to clarify. Reserve for later.

Over medium-high heat in a small saucepan, simmer WHITE PEPPER, VINEGAR, WATER and GHOST CHILI until the mixture is reduced by half. Place 6 EGG YOLKS in a steel bowl. Strain the vinegar mixture into the EGGS YOLKS. Cook EGG YOLKS over a double boiler, stirring constantly until the whisk starts to leave a trail in the eggs.. Immediately whip in LEMON JUICE and remove from heat.

Slowly whip in CLARIFIED BUTTER drop by drop until an emulsion is formed. Continue to slowly whip in CLARIFIED BUTTER until it is all incorporated. Season with SEA SALT, WHITE PEPPER and CAYENNE PEPPER. Keep HOLLANDAISE SAUCE warm.

In a small pan over high heat, fry CANADIAN BACON. In a pot of almost boiling water, poach EGGS and reserve. Toast ENGLISH MUFFINS. Plate the ENGLISH MUFFIN with CANADIAN BACON on top. Place poached EGGS on the BACON and top with HOLLANDAISE. Season with SEA SALT and BLACK PEPPER.

Yield: Serves 2.

Ingredient List

- (12 oz) Butter
- (1/2 tsp) White Pepper
- (3 oz) White Wine Vinegar
- (2 oz) Water
- (1 tbsp, minced) Ghost Chili
- (10) Eggs
- (1 1/2 oz) Lemon Juice
- (1 tsp) Sea Salt
- (1 tsp) Cayenne Pepper
- (4 slices) Canadian Bacon
- (2, split) English Muffins
- (1 tsp) Black Pepper

Ghostpacho
A fresh and vibrant chilled vegetable soup

Method

Place serving bowls in freezer to chill until service. Reserve some of the DICED VEGETABLES for garnishing each bowl.

In a blender, puree the TOMATO, ONION, GREEN and RED BELL PEPPERS, CUCUMBERS, GARLIC, RED WINE VINEGAR, LEMON JUICE, OLIVE OIL, GHOST CHILI, GHOST CHILI SAUCE, BREAD CRUMBS, GREEN ONION and BASIL until smooth.

Season with KOSHER SALT, BLACK PEPPER and CAYENNE PEPPER. Pulse in blender to incorporate.

Stir in the TOMATO JUICE, adding more to adjust the consistency to your liking.

Serve in chilled bowls and garnish the top of each bowl with fresh BASIL and the reserved DICED VEGETABLES.

Yield: Makes 8 servings.

Ingredient List

- (2 1/2 lbs) Tomatoes
- (1 large, diced) Red Onion
- (1, diced) Green Bell Pepper
- (1, diced) Red Bell Pepper
- (1 lb, diced) Cucumber
- (3 cloves, minced) Garlic
- (2 oz) Red Wine Vinegar
- (2 oz) Lemon Juice
- (4 oz) Olive Oil
- (2, diced) Ghost Chili
- (2 tbsp) Ghost Chili Sauce
- (3 oz) Bread Crumbs
- (1/2 cup, chopped) Green Onions
- (15 leaves, shredded) Basil
- (2 tbsp) Kosher Salt
- (1 tbsp) Black Pepper
- (1 tbsp) Cayenne Pepper
- (3 cups) Tomato Juice

Sriracha Sauce

A glowing orange thai and vietnamese condiment used to liven up any dish

Method

Place ALL INGREDIENTS into a small saucepan.
Bring to a boil and then lower to a simmer for 5 minutes.

Remove from the heat and allow the sauce
to come down to room temperature.

Transfer the sauce into a blender and puree for about 10 minutes.
If the mixture is too chunky and isn't pureeing well,
add in a teaspoon of water.

Taste the sauce and season it as needed.
Use a little SALT if it's too sweet. A little SUGAR if it's too tangy.

Allow the flavor to bloom for at least 5 hours before use.

Yield: Makes roughly 1 cup.

Ingredient List

- (1 lb) **Thai Chili**
- (4 cloves, minced) **Garlic**
- (3 tbsp) **Sugar**
- (1/4th cup) **White Vinegar**
- (1/2 cup) **Water**
- (1 1/2 tsp) **Salt**

For a few dollars you could buy the brand that you see in supermarkets, but the extra time and money to make it at home is worth it.

This sauce tastes much more fresh and spicy - without any of the additives.

Truly Deviled Eggs
Deviled eggs that actually live up to their name

Method

Turn EGGS over on their side to allow yolks to settle.

In medium bowl, combine MUSTARD, GHOST CHILI, WHITE VINEGAR, LIGHT MAYONNAISE, SALT and BLACK PEPPER to create the FILLING.

In a large pot filled with cool water, add EGGS.
Turn heat to high and allow eggs to boil for 7 minutes.

Remove EGGS and set aside to cool.
Gently tap EGGS to crack shell.

Peel EGGS and slice down the middle.
Remove EGG YOLK from eggs and stir into FILLING.
Pipe FILLING into EGGS.

Sprinkle with CAYENNE PEPPER and garnish with ITALIAN PARSLEY.

Yield: Makes 24 Truly Deviled Eggs.

Ingredient List

- (12) Eggs
- (2 tsp) Mustard
- (1 tbsp) Ghost Chili
- (2 tsp) White Vinegar
- (1 cup) Light Mayonnaise
- (1/2 tsp) Salt
- (1 tsp) Black Pepper
- (garnish) Cayenne Pepper
- (4 tbsp) Italian Parsley

For Whom The Bell Tolls

A sweet bell pepper stuffed with rice, beef and the hottest peppers in the world

Preparation

Preheat oven to 350 degrees.
Cut top off of RED BELL PEPPERS and hollow out peppers.

Method

In a large pot, combine 2 cups RICE and 2 1/2 cups water. Cover and bring to a boil. Turn off heat and allow RICE to finish absorbing water, about 10 minutes. Fluff with a fork.

In a large pan over medium heat pour in GHOST OIL. Add GARLIC and saute until golden brown (about 2 minutes). To the pan, add GROUND BEEF, CHOCOLATE HABANERO, GHOST CHILI, DEVIL'S TONGUE CHILI and HABANERO. Saute until BEEF is browned (about 5 minutes).

Add RICE to the pan and season with BLACK PEPPER and SEA SALT. Stir in OREGANO and ITALIAN PARSLEY.
Fill hollowed out RED BELL PEPPERS with BEEF and RICE mixture. Replace removed BELL PEPPER top.
Place STUFFED BELL PEPPERS on a baking sheet and bake for 10 minutes.

Yield: Makes 4 stuffed bell peppers.

Ingredient List

- (4 large) Red Bell Pepper
- (2 cups) Rice
- (2 tbsp) Ghost Oil [or Olive Oil]
- (3 cloves, minced) Garlic
- (1 lb) Ground Beef
- (2, minced) Chocolate Habanero
- (1, minced) Ghost Chili
- (1, minced) Devil's Tongue Chili
- (1, minced) Habanero
- (1 tbsp) Black Pepper
- (1 tbsp) Sea Salt
- (1 tbsp) Oregano
- (2 tbsp, chopped) Italian Parsley

The star of this dish is really the variety of peppers that you use. Each individual flavor comes out into the rice and the beef which act as as a perfect foil for the heat.

Ghost Chili Truffles

Rich chili infused dark chocolate ganache coated with hazelnuts and cayenne

Method

Temper MILK CHOCOLATE by slowly melting over a double boiler. Chop DARK CHOCOLATE and BUTTER into small pieces and place into a large metal bowl.

In a small, dry pan over medium heat toast HAZELNUTS and chop roughly.

In small pot over high heat, bring HEAVY CREAM and whole GHOST CHILI to a boil.

Remove GHOST CHILI - for extra heat finely mince and add 1 tsp back into the cream. Pour HEAVY CREAM over the DARK CHOCOLATE and BUTTER. Stir until DARK CHOCOLATE and BUTTER is completely melted. Stir in the BRANDY to complete the GANACHE.

Pour the GANACHE into a shallow pan and chill until firm. Using a teaspoon, shape the GANACHE into rough balls and immediately dip the truffle into tempered MILK CHOCOLATE and coat with COCOA POWDER and CAYENNE PEPPER or coat with chopped HAZELNUTS.

Yield: Makes 60 Truffles.

Ingredient List

- (1 lb) Milk Chocolate
- (1 lb) Dark Chocolate
- (1/2 lb) Unsalted Butter
- (1/4th cup, crushed) Hazelnuts
- (8 oz) Heavy Cream
- (1, whole) Ghost Chili
- (2 oz) Brandy
- (1 cup) Cocoa Powder
- (3 tbsp) Cayenne Pepper

The very dark chocolate stands up well to the incredible heat of the Ghost Chili.

Bruschetta
Toasted garlic bread topped with a tangy, sweet and spicy tomato mixture

Method

Slice BAGUETTE and lightly drizzle OLIVE OIL on top of the pieces.
Smash a clove of GARLIC and rub onto baguette.
Toast BAGUETTE in oven or on grill until slightly crisp.

In a small bowl, mix together TOMATO, GARLIC, BASIL, SEA SALT, GHOST CHILI, BALSAMIC VINEGAR, MOZZARELLA CHEESE and BLACK PEPPER.

Top bread with Bruschetta mixture and serve.

Yield: Serves 4 as an appetizer.

Ingredient List

- (1) **French Baguette**
- (1 tbsp) **Olive Oil**
- (2 cloves, minced) **Garlic**
- (6, diced) **Tomatoes**
- (2 cloves, minced) **Garlic**
- (8 leaves, shredded) **Basil**
- (2 tsp) **Sea Salt**
- (3 tbsp, minced) **Ghost Chili**
- (1 tbsp) **Balsamic Vinegar**
- (1/4th cup) **Mozzarella Cheese**
- (1 tsp) **Black Pepper**

Mango Habanero Wings
Sweet and spicy wings with a caribbean flair

Method

Fill deep fryer with VEGETABLE OIL and preheat to 375 degrees.

In medium sauce pan over medium-high heat sauté MANGO.
Add HABANERO, GARLIC, JERK SEASONING and VINEGAR.
Season with SALT and BLACK PEPPER.
Sauté for 10 minutes.

Remove from heat and pour into a blender.
Blend for 5 minutes, or until smooth.
Add sauce back into the saucepan.

Add BUTTER and CILANTRO.
Stir until BUTTER is melted and incorporated.

Fry CHICKEN WINGS until golden brown (9-10 minutes).
Drain the CHICKEN WINGS and add into saucepan.
Roll the CHICKEN WINGS around in the sauce and remove.

Garnish with CILANTRO and small pieces of HABANERO.

Yield: Makes a dozen wings.

Ingredient List

- (for frying) **Vegetable Oil**
- (4 cups, diced) **Mango**
- (3, minced) **Habanero**
- (1 tsp, minced) **Garlic**
- (2 tbsp) **Jerk Seasoning**
- (1/4th cup) **Vinegar**
- (1 tsp) **Salt**
- (1 tsp) **Black Pepper**
- (1 tbsp) **Butter**
- (1 tbsp) **Cilantro**
- (12) **Chicken Wings**

Ghost Vodka Sauce and Penne with Prosciutto

A ghost chili spiked vodka and tomato cream sauce over pasta

Method

In a large pot over medium-high heat, add GHOST OIL. Saute WHITE ONION, GHOST CHILI and GARLIC for 3-5 minutes until fragrant. Pour in VODKA and simmer for 5 minutes.

Add DICED TOMATO, TOMATO PASTE and simmer for 3 minutes. Pour in HEAVY CREAM and add in PARMESAN and ROMANO CHEESE. Allow to simmer for 20 minutes.

Stir in PROSCIUTTO and add OREGANO, BASIL and ITALIAN PARSLEY.

Season with BLACK PEPPER and 2 tsp KOSHER SALT.

In large pot over high heat, add 1 tbsp KOSHER SALT and fill with water. Allow water to reach rolling boil. Add PENNE and cook 6-8 minutes or until al Dente.

Drain and pour pasta into pot with GHOST VODKA SAUCE.

Stir to coat pasta with sauce and simmer for 2 minutes.

Yield: Serves 4.

Ingredient List

- (2 tbsp) Ghost Oil [or Olive Oil]
- (1, diced) White Onion
- (1, minced) Ghost Chili
- (6 cloves, minced) Garlic
- (1 1/4th cups) Vodka
- (29 oz) Diced Tomato
- (1 can) Tomato Paste
- (2 cups) Heavy Cream
- (1/4th cup) Parmesan Cheese
- (1/4th cup) Romano Cheese
- (3 oz, sliced) Prosciutto
- (2 tbsp) Oregano
- (5 leaves, shredded) Basil
- (2 tbsp, chopped) Italian Parsley
- (1 tsp) Black Pepper
- (2 tsp and 1 tbsp) Kosher Salt
- (1 lb) Penne

The vodka is essential – it draws out extra flavor from the cream and tomatoes.

Seared Salmon with Thai Sauce

Pan seared salmon in an herbaceous, thai-tanic sauce served over jasmine rice

Method

In a small saucepan over medium-high heat, combine COCONUT MILK, CLAM JUICE, LIME JUICE, FISH SAUCE, GINGER, GARLIC and THAI CHILIES. Bring the sauce to a simmer and cook down to 1 cup (about 10 minutes).

Season the SALMON with SEA SALT and BLACK PEPPER. In large pot over high heat, add 3 cups of WATER and 3 cups of JASMINE RICE. Bring to a rolling boil and turn heat off. Cover the pot with a lid until rest of the dish is complete.

Add the CILANTRO and GREEN ONION to the sauce.
Season the sauce with SEA SALT and BLACK PEPPER.
In a large pan over high heat, sear the SALMON for 1 ½ minutes.
Carefully flip the SALMON and sear the other side.
Turn down heat to medium and coat fish with 1/4th of the sauce.
Add BUTTER to the pan and baste the SALMON constantly.
Cook SALMON for 4 minutes on each side..
Uncover JASMINE RICE and fluff with fork.

Serve the SALMON over a bed of JASMINE RICE and pour reserved sauce over the SALMON and RICE.

Yield: Serves 4.

Ingredient List

- (1 cup) Coconut Milk
- (8 oz) Clam Juice
- (2 tbsp) Lime Juice
- (1 tsp) Fish Sauce
- (2 tsp) Ginger
- (2 cloves, minced) Garlic
- (3, sliced) Thai Chili
- (4 filets) Salmon
- (2 tsp) Sea Salt
- (2 tsp) Black Pepper
- (3 cups) Water
- (3 cups) Jasmine Rice
- (4 tbsp, chopped) Cilantro
- (4 tbsp, chopped) Green Onion
- (1/4 cup) Butter

Fool's Gold Sauce

A sultry, indian spiced devil's tongue and pineapple hot sauce

Method

In large pot over high heat, combine YELLOW TOMATO, PINEAPPLE and DEVIL'S TONGUE.
Simmer for 5 minutes.

Add VINEGAR, GARLIC POWDER, TURMERIC, GARAM MASALA and CURRY POWDER.

Season with WHITE PEPPER and SEA SALT.

Simmer for 25 minutes.

Remove from the pot in small batches and place in a blender. Blend until smooth (about 5 minutes per batch).

Yield: Makes 48 oz.

Ingredient List

- (12 large, diced) Yellow Tomato
- (1 whole, diced) Pineapple
- (15) Devil's Tongue Chili
- (1/4th cup) Vinegar
- (1 tbsp) Garlic Powder
- (1 tbsp) Turmeric
- (3 tbsp) Garam Masala
- (1 tbsp) Curry Powder
- (3 tbsp) White Pepper
- (2 tsp) Sea Salt

This sauce is a great blend of sweet and spicy. Use it as a marinade for fish, chicken and pork. It is a hit as a dip, too!

Banh Mi with Pickled Carrots and Daikon

A classic vietnamese sandwich with marinated pork and pickled vegetables

Preparation

Thinly slice PORK LOIN.
Slice THAI CHILIES and chop CILANTRO.
Mix SRIRACHA SAUCE into MAYONNAISE and refrigerate.

In a small pan over medium-high heat, combine WATER, SUGAR, RICE WINE VINEGAR, 1 tsp FISH SAUCE and GHOST CHILI. Bring to a boil and remove from heat. In small glass bowl, add the liquid mixture, CARROT and DAIKON. Lightly season with KOSHER SALT and allow mixture to refrigerate for at least an hour (overnight is best).

In a food processor, combine GARLIC, SHALLOTS, 2 tsp FISH SAUCE, BLACK PEPPER, VEGETABLE OIL, LIME JUICE and GHOST CHILI SAUCE. Pulse to create marinade. Add mixture to PORK LOIN and marinate overnight.

Method

In medium pan over high heat, saute PORK LOIN slices until crispy. Spread SRIRACHA MAYO on CRISPY BAGUETTES and build Banh Mi with CUCUMBER, PORK, DAIKON & CARROT, CILANTRO and THAI CHILIES.
Yield: Makes 4 half sandwiches.

Ingredient List

- (1 lb) Pork Loin
- (garnish) Thai Chili
- (garnish) Cilantro
- (2 tbsp) Sriracha Sauce
- (1/2 cup) Mayonnaise
- (1/2 cup) Water
- (1/4th cup) Sugar
- (1/4th cup) Rice Wine Vinegar
- (3 tsp) Fish Sauce
- (1, diced) Ghost Chili
- (1/2 cup, julienne) Carrot
- (1/2 cup, julienne) Daikon Radish
- (1/4th tsp) Kosher Salt
- (4 cloves, minced) Garlic
- (2 tbsp, minced) Shallots
- (2 tsp) Black Pepper
- (1/4th cup) Vegetable Oil
- (2 tbsp) Lime Juice
- (1 tbsp) Ghost Chili Sauce
- (2) Crispy Baguette
- (1/2 cup, julienne) Cucumber

These Fries Aren't From France

Crispy, golden fries double fried in ghost oil and served with spicy condiments

Method

Add GHOST OIL to deep fryer and preheat to 350 degrees.
Rinse off RUSSET POTATOES.
Slice POTATOES into desired shape.

Whip SRIRACHA SAUCE into MAYONNAISE to create SRIRACHA MAYO.

Mix KETCHUP, CURRY POWDER and GHOST CHILI SAUCE to create CURRY KETCHUP.

Drop sliced POTATOES into the fryer. Fry for 3 minutes.
Remove and drain, allow to sit for 2 minutes.

Bring oil to 375 degrees.
Deep fry the POTATOES until golden and crispy (about 2 minutes).
Remove and drain.

Season with KOSHER SALT, BLACK PEPPER and GARLIC POWDER.

Serve with SRIRACHA MAYO and CURRY KETCHUP.

Yield: Makes 4 servings.

Ingredient List

- (for deep frying) Ghost Oil
- (2 1/2 lbs) Russet Potatoes
- (2 tbsp) Sriracha Sauce
- (1/2 cup) Mayonnaise
- (1/2 cup) Ketchup
- (2 tsp) Curry Powder
- (1 tbsp) Ghost Chili Sauce
- (1 tbsp) Kosher Salt
- (1 tbsp) Black Pepper
- (2 tsp) Garlic Powder

It is amazing how much flavor and heat the Ghost Oil gives when frying.

Serve these crispy, fries with the Sriracha Mayo and Curry Ketchup and you'll have some happy guests.

Sausage and Swiss Chard Pasta

A light, refreshing sausage pasta injected with ghost chili and fresh herbs

Preparation

Rinse SWISS CHARD and slice into thin strips, discarding the stalk.
Remove casing from ITALIAN SAUSAGE.
In large pot over high heat, bring water to rolling boil.
Add 1 tbsp SALT to water.

Method

In pan over medium heat, add 2 tbsp of OLIVE OIL.
Saute GARLIC until golden brown and aromatic.
Add GHOST CHILI and sauté for two minutes.
Add ITALIAN SAUSAGE and sauté until lightly browned.
Stir in ROSEMARY, THYME and OREGANO.

Add SWISS CHARD to the boiling water for 1 minute.
Add FETTUCCINE to boiling water and cook until al dente (6 minutes).

Drain FETTUCCINE and SWISS CHARD. Combine SAUSAGE mixture with PASTA, SWISS CHARD and PARMESAN.

Toss PASTA with 4 tbsp of OLIVE OIL.
Season with SALT and PEPPER.

Yield: Serves 4.

Ingredient List

(1 lb) Swiss Chard
(1 lb) Sweet Italian Sausage
(1 tsp) Kosher Salt
(6 tbsp) Olive Oil
(3 cloves, minced) Garlic
(1 tbsp, minced) Ghost Chili
(1 tsp) Rosemary
(2 tsp) Thyme
(1 tsp) Oregano
(1 lb) Fettuccine
(1/2 cup) Parmesan Cheese

This is an easy to make, quick dinner that is very flavorful and inexpensive.

Shrimp and Scallop Ceviche

Chilled shellfish cured in lime juice and served with fresh herbs and vegetables

Preparation

Peel and de-vein SHRIMP.
Chop SCALLOPS and SHRIMP into very similar pieces.

Place into a non-reactive container (Plastic, Glass or Stainless Steel).
Add LIME JUICE.
Cover and marinate in the refrigerator for 4 hours or
until the SHRIMP and SCALLOPS turn opaque and become firm.

Method

Remove the SHRIMP and SCALLOPS from the refrigerator.
Add the THAI CHILIES, CILANTRO, GARLIC, TOMATO
and RED ONION and OLIVE OIL.

Mix well until all ingredients are incorporated.

Adjust seasoning with SEA SALT and BLACK PEPPER.

Return to the refrigerator to cool and serve within 2 hours.

Yield: Serves 8.

Ingredient List

- (1 lb) **Shrimp**
- (1 lb) **Sea Scallops**
- (10 oz) **Lime Juice**
- (3, sliced) **Thai Chili**
- (4 tbsp, chopped) **Cilantro**
- (2 tsp, minced) **Garlic**
- (8 oz) **Diced Tomato**
- (1, diced) **Red Onion**
- (1 oz) **Olive Oil**
- (1 tsp) **Sea Salt**
- (1 tsp) **Black Pepper**

Chicken Panang Curry

A golden, spicy thai curry sauce swimming with chicken and vegetables

Method

Heat large wok or non-stick pan over medium heat. Add SUGAR into the wok and allow it to liquefy.

Add PANANG CURRY PASTE, GARLIC and GINGER and constantly stir until fragrant (about 2 minutes).

Add sliced CHICKEN BREAST and saute until golden brown, about 4 minutes.

Pour in COCONUT MILK and CHICKEN STOCK and gently simmer for 5 minutes.

Add BAMBOO SHOOTS and CARROT, simmer for 3 minutes.

Stir in FISH SAUCE and KAFFIR LIME LEAVES.

Add RED BELL PEPPER and simmer for 5 minutes. Season with SALT and stir in THAI BASIL and THAI CHILIES.

Yield: Serves 4.

Ingredient List

- (1 tbsp) Sugar
- (2 oz) Panang Curry Paste
- (2 cloves, minced) Garlic
- (1 tsp, minced) Ginger
- (1 lb, sliced) Chicken Breasts
- (12 oz) Coconut Milk
- (8 oz) Chicken Stock
- (12 oz) Bamboo Shoots
- (1 1/2 cup, julienne) Carrot
- (1 tbsp) Fish Sauce
- (4, minced) Kaffir Lime Leaves [or 2 TBSP Lime Zest]
- (1, sliced) Red Bell Pepper
- (2 tsp) Kosher Salt
- (10 leaves, shredded) Thai Basil
- (5, sliced) Thai Chili

Grilled Caribbean Flank Steak with Mo'Jolokia Sauce
Marinated flank steak covered in a fresh ghost chili mojo sauce

Preparation

Create marinade by combining SOY SAUCE, GINGER, HONEY, GHOST OIL. 2 cloves GARLIC, 1 tsp BLACK PEPPER, 1 tsp SALT, 1 GHOST CHILI and 1 tsp OREGANO in a food processor.

Pour marinade into a plastic bag and add FLANK STEAK. Close and refrigerate overnight.

Create Mo'Jolokia Sauce by combining 2 cloves GARLIC, WHITE ONION, ORANGE JUICE, LIME JUICE, CUMIN, 1 tsp OREGANO, 1 tsp BLACK PEPPER, 1 tsp SALT, OLIVE OIL, 1 GHOST CHILI and CILANTRO into a food processor. Pulse until smooth.
Cover and refrigerate sauce overnight.

Method

Preheat grill to a high temperature. Place FLANK STEAK onto the grate and grill for about 6 minutes per side.

Remove from grill and cover, allowing meat to rest for 5 minutes. Serve topped with Mo'Jolokia Sauce.

Yield: Serves 4.

Ingredient List

- (1/4th cup) **Soy Sauce**
- (1 tbsp) **Ginger**
- (1 tbsp) **Honey**
- (3 tsp) **Ghost Oil** [or Olive Oil]
- (4 cloves, minced) **Garlic**
- (2 tsp) **Black Pepper**
- (2 tsp) **Kosher Salt**
- (2, minced) **Ghost Chili**
- (2 tsp) **Oregano**
- (1 lb) **Flank Steak**
- (3 tbsp, diced) **White Onion**
- (1/3rd cup) **Orange Juice**
- (3 tbsp) **Lime Juice**
- (1 tsp) **Cumin**
- (1/3rd cup) **Olive Oil**
- (4 tbsp) **Cilantro**

Trio of Chili Sorbets
Three powerful fruit sorbets electrified with chili peppers

Preparation

Place three small, square, glass baking dishes in the freezer to chill.

In a small pot over medium-high heat, add WATER and SUGAR. Whisk until SUGAR is dissolved into the water and simmer for about 10 minutes to create the SIMPLE SYRUP.

Method

In a blender, add 1/4th cup SIMPLE SYRUP along with PINEAPPLE and DEVIL'S TONGUE. Add in 1 tbsp LEMON JUICE and blend for 5-6 minutes or until completely smooth.
Repeat the same steps with the GHOST CHILI and CRANBERRY and then the MANGO and CHOCOLATE HABANERO.

Remove the glass dishes from the freezer and spread each mixture into a thin, even layer. Place in freezer.
Every 15 minutes, stir mixtures with a fork, breaking up the ice crystals that form. Remove from freezer when mixture is fully frozen.
If a smoother texture is desired, place mixture into a food processor and pulse to break up large ice crystals.

Yield: Serves 4.

Ingredient List

(1 cup) **Water**
(1 cup) **Sugar**
(1 1/2 cup, diced) **Pineapple**
(1/2 pepper) **Devil's Tongue**
(3 tbsp) **Lemon Juice**
(1) **Ghost Chili**
(1 1/2 cup) **Cranberry**
(2 cups) **Mango**
(1) **Chocolate Habanero**

There is something very invigorating about eating a frozen, refreshing sorbet while at the same time, having your taste buds awakened by the intense heat of the peppers.

Clams Casino

A succulent and amped up classic preparation of half shell clams

Method

Preheat Oven to 400 degrees.
In a medium pan over high heat, fry the BACON until well done.
Reserve 2 tbsp of the bacon fat and drain the rest.
Crumble the BACON into small pieces.

In the same pan, lower the heat to medium-high and add in bacon fat.
Sauté the GARLIC, RED BELL PEPPER, GHOST CHILI, and ONION until tender (3-5 minutes).

Set aside the GARLIC, GHOST CHILI, PEPPER and ONION to cool.
Add the softened BUTTER, LEMON JUICE, ITALIAN PARSLEY, WORCESTERSHIRE SAUCE and BACON to the vegetables.
Stir until the BUTTER is well incorporated and add in the PANKO.
Transfer to a glass bowl and season with KOSHER SALT and BLACK PEPPER. Refrigerate until needed.

In a medium pan over high heat, add the CLAMS with water and cover to steam until opened. Discard the top shell of the clam.
Fill the remaining half with 1 tsp of the filling mixture.
Place CLAMS onto a metal baking sheet and bake in the oven for 10 minutes (or until browned). Garnish with OREGANO.

Yield: Makes 24 Clams Casino.

Ingredient List

(4 slices, diced) **Bacon**
(1 tbsp, minced) **Garlic**
(3 tbsp, diced) **Red Bell Pepper**
(1 tsp) **Ghost Chili**
(4 tbsp, diced) **Onion**
(4 oz, softened) **Butter**
(1 tbsp) **Lemon Juice**
(2 tbsp chopped) **Italian Parsley**
(2 tsp) **Worcestershire Sauce**
(2 tbsp) **Panko Breadcrumbs**
(1/4th tsp) **Kosher Salt**
(1/4th tsp) **Black Pepper**
(24, scrubbed) **Clams**
(garnish) **Oregano**

The Ghost Chili, when used lightly, really compliments shellfish nicely.

Cuban Missile Crisis Burgers with Ghost Chili Relish
The flavor and fire of cuban cuisine resonate throughout this juicy burger

Method

Pre-heat your grill to medium-high temperature. Combine PICKLE RELISH, GHOST CHILI, DIJON MUSTARD and YELLOW MUSTARD to make "Ghost Chili Relish".

In large bowl, combine GROUND BEEF, GARLIC, CHILI POWDER, CUMIN, CILANTRO and GHOST CHILI SAUCE. Season with SEA SALT and BLACK PEPPER.

Divide into four equal portions and form even patties. Allow burgers to cool in fridge for at least 15 minutes. If you leave them overnight, the flavors will further develop and marry together.

Place patties on the grill and cook 5 minutes on each side, or to your preference. Before the burgers are done, flip them a second time and add a slice of HAM and a slice of MONTERREY JACK. Cook until the cheese is well melted. Toast the HAMBURGER BUNS by placing them on the grill for 30 seconds.

On the top and bottom halves of the bun, spread a generous amount of the GHOST CHILI RELISH. Add burgers and additional toppings.

Yield: Makes 4 quarter pound burgers.

Ingredient List

- (1/4th cup) Sweet Pickle Relish
- (2 tbsp, minced) Ghost Chili
- (1/4th cup) Dijon Mustard
- (1/4th cup) Yellow Mustard
- (1 lb) Ground Beef
- (3 cloves, minced) Garlic
- (1 tsp) Chili Powder
- (1 tsp) Cumin
- (2 tbsp) Cilantro
- (2 tbsp) Ghost Chili Sauce
- (1 tsp) Kosher Salt
- (2 tsp) Black Pepper
- (4 slices) Ham
- (4 slices) Monterrey Jack
- (4) Hamburger Buns

Thai Fried Rice
Egg fried jasmine rice with vegetables and thai flavors

Preparation
Cook the JASMINE RICE (4 cups rice, 4 cups water). Remove and chill for 30 minutes.

Method
Heat a wok over medium-high heat and add VEGETABLE OIL. Add the GINGER and GARLIC and stir-fry until lightly browned and fragrant. Remove from the pan and reserve.

Add the CARROTS, YELLOW PEPPER and ONION, stir-fry until tender and remove.

Add in the RICE and stir-fry until warmed through. Make a well in the center of the RICE and pour in the EGGS. Cook until the EGGS are almost set before mixing them into the RICE. Add in the TOMATOES, GARLIC, GINGER and STIR FRIED VEGETABLES.

Stir in the LIME JUICE, THAI CHILIES, CILANTRO, THAI BASIL and FISH SAUCE. Season with SALT and BLACK PEPPER. Stir-fry until hot and serve.

Yield: Serves 4.

Ingredient List
- (4 cups) Jasmine Rice
- (3 oz) Vegetable Oil
- (1 tbsp) Ginger
- (3 tbsp) Garlic
- (1 cup, julienne) Carrot
- (1 cup, sliced) Yellow Bell Pepper
- (1 cup, diced) Onion
- (5, diced) Thai Chili
- (2) Eggs
- (1 1/2 cups) Diced Tomato
- (1 tbsp) Lime Juice
- (2 tbsp) Cilantro
- (3 tbsp) Fish Sauce
- (1 tbsp) Kosher Salt
- (1/2 tsp) Black Pepper
- (10 leaves, shredded) Thai Basil

Ghost Chili Bolognese
A thermonuclear take on a mouth-watering classic Italian beef ragù

Method

In large pan over medium heat, add BUTTER and GHOST OIL.

Sauté CARROT, CELERY, GARLIC and ONION until vegetables are soft (about 6 minutes).

Add GROUND BEEF and GHOST CHILI and sauté until browned. Pour in WHITE WINE and cook off until pan is nearly dry. Add NUTMEG to MILK and pour into pan. Cook until nearly dry. Add DICED TOMATOES and sauté for 5 minutes.

Turn heat to low and simmer for 2-3 hours, occasionally adding CHICKEN STOCK and stirring to keep sauce from sticking to pan.

Season with KOSHER SALT and GROUND BLACK PEPPER Stir in ITALIAN PARSLEY.

Serve over a bed of pasta and top with fresh Parmesan cheese.

Yield: Serves 4.

Ingredient List

- (1 oz) Butter
- (2 oz) Ghost Oil [or Olive Oil]
- (1 1/2, julienne) Carrot
- (4 ribs, diced) Celery
- (6 cloves, minced) Garlic
- (1/2 large, diced) Onion
- (1 lb) Ground Beef
- (2, minced) Ghost Chili
- (8 oz) White Wine
- (2 tsp) Nutmeg
- (6 oz) Milk
- (29 oz) Diced Tomatoes
- (26 oz) Chicken Stock
- (2 tsp) Kosher Salt
- (2 tsp) Black Pepper
- (1/4 cup, chopped) Italian Parsley

This sauce will reward the time, love and patience that you put into it.

Pineapple Ravioli with Devil's Tongue

A refreshing pineapple "ravioli" stuffed with cream cheese and blackberry

Preparation

In a small pan over high heat, pour in BALSAMIC VINEGAR. Reduce mixture in half, or until it thickens to a glaze. Remove from heat, reserve and refrigerate the sauce until cooled.

In a small bowl, mix together the CREAM CHEESE, MINT, BLACKBERRY and DEVIL'S TONGUE PEPPER.

Cut the stem off of the PINEAPPLE and also trim the sides to make it square. Setting the PINEAPPLE on its side, cut the fruit into very thin sheets to act as the ravioli. Turn on broiler to "high" setting.

Method

On a non-stick baking sheet, place the first slice of PINEAPPLE and top with the CREAM CHEESE AND BLACKBERRY MIXTURE. Lay another thin slice of PINEAPPLE on top of the mixture and press the sides down to create the RAVIOLI. Broil for 1-2 minutes.

Paint the plate with the BALSAMIC VINEGAR REDUCTION and set the PINEAPPLE RAVIOLI down on top. Garnish with extra BLACKBERRIES, WHIPPED CREAM and MINT LEAVES.

Yield: Makes 6 servings.

Ingredient List

- (1/2 cup) **Balsamic Vinegar**
- (3/4 cup) **Cream Cheese**
- (2 tbsp and garnish) **Mint**
- (20) **Blackberry**
- (1 tbsp, minced) **Devil's Tongue**
- (1, whole) **Pineapple**
- (garnish) **Whipped Cream**

Don't be afraid to use the balsamic vinegar. As you reduce it, the sauce turns sweeter and perfectly compliments the fruit.

Take care not to over-reduce and burn the sauce!

Straight Razor Cocktail
A cranberry, vodka and ghost chili cocktail

Preparation

In a small jar add whole GHOST CHILI and VODKA. Cover and refrigerate overnight.

Method

In an ice filled shaker, combine GHOST VODKA, LIME JUICE and CRANBERRY JUICE.

Shake vigorously and strain into a highball glass.

Serve on the rocks and garnish with fresh CRANBERRIES, MINT LEAVES, a LIME WEDGE and a sliver of GHOST CHILI.

Yield: Makes 1 drink.

Ingredient List

- (1) Ghost Chili
- (3 oz) Vodka
- (2 tbsp) Lime Juice
- (5 oz) Cranberry Juice
- (2) Cranberries
- (garnish) Mint
- (garnish) Lime Wedge

A classic cocktail with a very unique twist.

The heat from the pepper compliments the tart cranberries and really gives the vodka a bite.

Scalloped Potatoes
Sliced potatoes baked in a fierce, sweet and salty cream sauce

Method

Preheat oven to 375 degrees.
Slice POTATOES into thin rounds.
In small bowl, combine HEAVY CREAM, CREAMED CORN and GHOST CHILI.

Season CREAM AND CORN MIXTURE with SALT and BLACK PEPPER.

In a 9x5 baking dish, arrange layer of POTATOES. Drizzle layer of HEAVY CREAM/CORN MIXTURE and add layer of HAM. Continue layering with POTATOES, HEAVY CREAM/CORN and HAM until reaching the top of the dish.

Top with MOZZARELLA CHEESE and cover with foil.
Bake for 45 minutes.
Remove the foil and bake for 5 minutes, or until cheese is golden brown.

Sprinkle CAYENNE PEPPER on top prior to serving.

Yield: Serves 4.

Ingredient List

(4 large, thinly sliced) **Potatoes**
(1/4th cup) **Heavy Cream**
(14 oz) **Creamed Corn**
(1 tbsp, minced) **Ghost Chili**
(3 tsp) **Kosher Salt**
(2 tsp) **Black Pepper**
(8 oz, diced) **Ham Steak**
(1/2 cup) **Mozzarella Cheese**
(1 tbsp) **Cayenne Pepper**

This is comfort food at its finest.

The sweetness of the corn and the smoky, salty ham play off of each other and enhance the chili infused cream.

Mussels and Chorizo

A preparation of mussels and chorizo in a scorching hot white wine sauce

Preparation

Rinse MUSSELS, scrub off any grit and remove "beard" if present.
Remove the casings from the CHORIZO.
Uncork and "test" the WHITE WINE to make sure it is delicious.
Discard MUSSELS that are open and do not close when tapped.

Method

Heat GHOST OIL in large pan.
Add CHORIZO and cook until barely browned.
Remove and drain off most of the grease.
Add ONION, GARLIC and GHOST CHILI.
Cook until ONION is softened and GARLIC is fragrant.

Add the CHORIZO back into the pot. Add MUSSELS and RED BELL PEPPER. Pour in WHITE WINE.
Allow the alcohol to cook off for about 45 seconds, then add PARSLEY, GREEN ONION, SALT and GHOST CHILI SAUCE.

Cover the MUSSELS and steam until opened (about 3 minutes).
Discard any MUSSELS that fail to open.
Serve in large bowl with CRUSTY BREAD.

Yield: Serves 2.

Ingredient List

- (2 lb) Mussels
- (8 oz) Chorizo
- (12 oz) White Wine
- (2 oz) Ghost Oil [or Olive Oil]
- (1/2, diced) Onion
- (4 cloves, minced) Garlic
- (2 tbsp, minced) Ghost Chili
- (1, diced) Red Bell Pepper
- (2 tbsp, chopped) Italian Parsley
- (4 tbsp, chopped) Green Onion
- (1 tsp) Salt
- (3 tbsp) Ghost Chili Sauce
- (4 pieces) Crusty Bread

Thai Hot Wings

Wings coated in a monsoon of sweet, sour and sweltering thai flavors

Preparation

Add VEGETABLE OIL to deep fryer and pre-heat to 375 degrees.

Method

In medium saucepan over high heat, combine SWEET CHILI SAUCE, FISH SAUCE, HONEY, SALT, PEPPER, VINEGAR, THAI CHILI and CILANTRO. Simmer for 10 minutes.

Drop CHICKEN WINGS into deep fryer and cook until golden brown and crispy (about 12 minutes).

Remove CHICKEN WINGS from fryer and drain.

Toss CHICKEN WINGS in the saucepan and serve. Garnish with extra THAI CHILIES and CILANTRO.

Yield: Makes 12 Thai Hot Wings.

Ingredient List

- (for frying) Vegetable Oil
- (1/2 cup) Sweet Chili Sauce
- (1 tsp) Fish Sauce
- (1 tbsp) Honey
- (1/2 tsp) Salt
- (1/4th tsp) Black Pepper
- (1/4th cup) Vinegar
- (5, sliced) Thai Chili
- (1 tbsp) Cilantro
- (12) Chicken Wings

These wings are great to have in your arsenal. They are simple to put together but contain sweet, spicy, sour and salty flavors.

These are a great way to mix things up at parties!

Fettuccine with Bacon, Goat Cheese and Roasted Asparagus

Roasted asparagus and pasta in a spicy, smoky goat cheese sauce

Preparation

Preheat oven to 450 degrees.
Fill large pot with water and season generously with KOSHER SALT.
Bring water to a rolling boil.

Method

Place ASPARAGUS on large baking sheet.
Top ASPARAGUS with 2 tbsp BUTTER, KOSHER SALT and
BLACK PEPPER. Roast in oven for 10-15 minutes, tossing occasionally.
Remove from oven and cut into 2 inch lengths.

Fry BACON, drain and crumble.
Add FETTUCCINE to boiling water and cook until al dente (7-8 minutes).
Keep 1 ½ cups of PASTA WATER and drain pasta and return to the pot.

In a small bowl, combine GOAT CHEESE, GHOST CHILI,
3 tbsp BUTTER and 2/3 cup PASTA WATER.
Season with SALT and PEPPER and whisk until smooth.
Add GOAT CHEESE MIXTURE, PARMESAN CHEESE, BACON
and ASPARAGUS to pasta. Toss to combine. Add more water if needed.
Garnish with GHOST CHILI and CHIVES.

Yield: Serves 4.

Ingredient List

(1 lb, trimmed) **Asparagus**
(5 tbsp) **Butter**
(to taste) **Kosher Salt**
(to taste) **Black Pepper**
(4 strips, diced) **Bacon**
(1 lb) **Fettuccine**
(5 oz) **Goat Cheese**
(1 tbsp, minced) **Ghost Chili**
(1/4th cup) **Parmesan Cheese**
(3 tbsp, chopped) **Chives**

Chicken Tikka Masala
Spiced yogurt marinated chicken in a spicy, sweet tomato cream sauce

Preparation

Create marinade by combining YOGURT, CARDAMOM, 1 GHOST CHILI , 2 tbsp GARAM MASALA and LEMON JUICE. Make several shallow slashes into the CHICKEN BREAST and place in a container with marinade. Set Broiler to High.

Method

In a medium saucepan over medium heat add VEGETABLE OIL. Add in WHITE ONION, GINGER, GHOST CHILI, and GARLIC. Saute until the garlic is golden and fragrant.

Stir in DICED TOMATOES, TOMATO SAUCE and HEAVY CREAM. Simmer for 10 minutes. Add in CUMIN, CORIANDER, TURMERIC, SUGAR, SALT, BLACK PEPPER, 2 tbsp GARAM MASALA, BUTTER and OREGANO. Simmer for 25 minutes.

Remove CHICKEN from marinade and remove excess. Place on baking sheet and broil in the oven until golden brown and cooked through. (10-12 minutes).

Remove CHICKEN from under the broiler, slice and add to TOMATO SAUCE. Serve with Rice or Naan bread.
Yield: Serves 4.

Ingredient List

- (6 oz) Yogurt
- (1 tbsp) Cardamom
- (2, minced) Ghost Chili
- (4 tbsp) Garam Masala
- (1 tbsp) Lemon Juice
- (2 lb) Chicken Breast
- (1 tbsp) Vegetable Oil
- (4 tbsp, diced) White Onion
- (1 tbsp, minced) Ginger
- (4 cloves, minced) Garlic
- (29 oz) Diced Tomatoes
- (1 cup) Tomato Sauce
- (12 oz) Heavy Cream
- (2 tbsp) Cumin
- (2 tbsp, crushed) Coriander Seed
- (2 tbsp) Turmeric
- (1/4th cup) Sugar
- (2 tsp) Kosher Salt
- (1 tbsp) Black Pepper
- (1 tbsp) Butter
- (1 tbsp) Oregano

Steak Die-Anne

Pan fried new york strip steaks coated in a creamy ghost chili cognac sauce

Method

Coat STEAKS with KOSHER SALT and cracked BLACK PEPPERCORNS.

In medium pan over high heat melt BUTTER. Turn heat to medium high and add STEAKS, GARLIC and SHALLOTS. Cook for 3-4 minutes, constantly basting with BUTTER. Flip and cook for another 3-4 minutes, constantly basting. Remove STEAKS and hold in warm oven.

Pour COGNAC in pan and carefully ignite. Cook off alcohol and add HEAVY CREAM. Stir in diced MUSHROOMS. Add DIJON MUSTARD, GHOST CHILI and WORCESTERSHIRE SAUCE.

Stir in ITALIAN PARSLEY, TARRAGON, and GHOST CHILI SAUCE. Add STEAKS back into pan and simmer for 1 minute.

Flip the STEAKS to coat in the sauce and simmer for an additional minute.

Yield: Serves 2.

Ingredient List

- (2) NY Strip Steak
- (2 tbsp) Kosher Salt
- (4 tbsp) Black Peppercorns
- (1 tbsp) Butter
- (2 cloves, minced) Garlic
- (2, minced) Shallots
- (1/3rd cup) Cognac
- (1/2 cup) Heavy Cream
- (10, diced) White Mushrooms
- (1 tbsp) Dijon Mustard
- (1, minced) Ghost Chili
- (1 tbsp) Worcestershire Sauce
- (1/4th cup, minced) Italian Parsley
- (1 tbsp) Tarragon
- (2 tbsp) Ghost Chili Sauce

Careful use of Ghost Chilies can elevate classic dishes without becoming too overbearing.

Coconut Milk and Mango Panna Cotta

A heavenly mango and coconut milk treat with thai chilies and raspberries

Preparation

Coat 6 ramekins with NON-STICK BAKING SPRAY and set aside. In a small cup, pour in ORANGE JUICE and sprinkle GELATIN over the juice. Keep aside to allow gelatin to bloom.

In separate bowl, whisk YOGURT and MANGO PUREE to combine.

In a medium saucepan over medium heat, combine COCONUT CREAM, HEAVY CREAM, LEMON ZEST, SUGAR, and BASIL. Simmer for 3 minutes, but do not allow cream to boil. Remove from heat and remove BASIL from mixture.

Create an ice bath by filling large bowl with ice. In a smaller bowl, pour in the COCONUT CREAM mixture and place that bowl into the ice bath. Stir in gelatin until completely dissolved. Add YOGURT and MANGO PUREE to CREAM MIXTURE and whisk in until cool. Pour into the ramekins and chill in the refrigerator for 4 hours.

In a small bowl, crush RASPBERRIES and stir in LIME JUICE and THAI CHILIES.
Remove ramekins and with a thin knife, loosen edges of the Panna Cotta. Top Panna Cotta with RASPBERRY AND CHILI MIXTURE.

Yield: Serves 6

Ingredient List

- Non-stick Baking Spray
- (4 tbsp) Orange Juice
- (1 packet) Gelatin
- (1 container) Vanilla Yogurt
- (1 cup) Mango Puree
- (1 cup) Coconut Cream
- (1/2 cup) Heavy Cream
- (1 tbsp) Lemon Zest
- (3/4th cup) Sugar
- (2 leaves, chopped) Basil
- (1/4th cup) Raspberries
- (1 tsp) Lime Juice
- (2, minced) Thai Chili

Don't put the mixture into the ramekins until you are sure it is cooled – the results will not be nearly as tasty.

Ghost Chili Pizza

Ghost chili pizza dough topped with sausage, red peppers and basil

Preparation

Place 4 oz warm WATER in a small dish. Sprinkle ACTIVE DRY YEAST into the dish and allow it to bloom for 5 minutes.

In a stand mixer, use the dough hook to combine FLOUR, SALT, GHOST CHILI, 4 oz cool WATER, YEAST / WATER MIX, HONEY, and OLIVE OIL to create GHOST CHILI DOUGH. Mix until you get a doughy texture. Remove dough from the mixer, cover and allow it to sit at room temperature for 30 minutes.

Preheat oven to 375 degrees.

Method

In a food processor, create pizza sauce by combining THYME, 5 leaves BASIL, DICED TOMATOES and OREGANO. Remove SAUSAGE from casings. In a small pan over high heat, saute ITALIAN SAUSAGE until lightly browned.

Stretch out DOUGH and ladle PIZZA SAUCE onto it. Add MOZZARELLA CHEESE, RED BELL PEPPER, crumbled ITALIAN SAUSAGE and 5 leaves BASIL to complete. Bake for 12 minutes.

Yield: Serves 4.

Ingredient List

- (8 oz) Water
- (1 tbsp) Active Dry Yeast
- (14 oz) Flour
- (1 tsp) Salt
- (2, minced) Ghost Chili
- (1 tbsp) Honey
- (2 tbsp) Olive Oil
- (2 tbsp) Thyme
- (10 leaves, shredded) Basil
- (14.5 oz) Diced Tomatoes
- (2 tbsp) Oregano
- (1 lb) Sweet Italian Sausage
- (1, diced) Red Bell Pepper
- (2 cups) Mozzarella Cheese

A shortcut is to purchase pre-made pizza dough and kneed in the ghost chili.

Pineapple, Ham and Devil's Tongue make for great toppings, too! Experiment!

Stuffed French Toast with Spicy Syrup

Crowned with ghost chili syrup and stuffed with raspberries and mascarpone

Method

In small bowl, combine CREAM CHEESE, MASCARPONE CHEESE, POWDERED SUGAR, RASPBERRIES, SALT and LEMON ZEST. Stir to mix together.

In medium-sized rectangular dish, add MILK, EGGS, CINNAMON, WHITE SUGAR and NUTMEG. Lightly whisk to incorporate EGGS. In small glass container, combine GHOST CHILI and MAPLE SYRUP. Cover and refrigerate until needed.

In a medium-sized pan over medium heat, melt BUTTER. As BUTTER melts, dip each piece of BREAD into the MILK AND EGG BATTER. Flip and cover both sides.

Add battered BREAD to pan and fry to golden brown, flipping once. Remove from pan and place on a paper towel to drain. Reserve in a warm oven until all of the FRENCH TOAST is created.

Layer once piece of FRENCH TOAST and cover with the filling. Place the second piece of FRENCH TOAST on top. Dust with POWDERED SUGAR, garnish with RASPBERRIES and pour the CHILI-INFUSED MAPLE SYRUP over top.

Yield: Serves 4.

Ingredient List

- (4 oz) Cream Cheese
- (4 oz) Mascarpone Cheese
- (2 tbsp) Powdered Sugar
- (8 oz) Raspberries
- (1/8th tsp) Salt
- (1 tsp) Lemon Zest
- (1 cup) Milk
- (3) Eggs
- (1/2 tbsp) Cinnamon
- (1 tbsp) White Sugar
- (1/4th tsp) Nutmeg
- (2 tsp, minced) Ghost Chili
- (3/4ths cup) Maple Syrup
- (4 tbsp) Butter
- (8 slices) Dense White Bread

Voodoo Chili

A satisfyingly complex, hallucinogenic beef and sausage chili

Method

In large crock pot, combine TOMATO SAUCE, DICED TOMATOES, BEEF STOCK, CHILI POWDER, CUMIN and BLACK PEPPER.

Turn heat to high and simmer.

In large pot over medium heat, pour in GHOST OIL. Saute GARLIC until golden brown (about 2 minutes). Remove casings from ITALIAN SAUSAGE. Add in GROUND BEEF and ITALIAN SAUSAGE. Saute until lightly browned. Add GARLIC, BEEF and SAUSAGE to crock pot.

Add CHOCOLATE HABANERO, GREEN BELL PEPPER, HABANERO, JALAPENO, DEVIL'S TONGUE, and GHOST CHILI to the crock pot.

Stir in DARK CHOCOLATE until melted.

Allow chili to simmer for 4-6 hours. Season with KOSHER SALT and stir in CILANTRO. Serve with tortilla chips and shredded cheese.

Yield: Serves 8.

Ingredient List

- (14.5 oz) Tomato Sauce
- (29 oz) Diced Tomatoes
- (16 oz) Beef Stock
- (4 tbsp) Chili Powder
- (2 tbsp) Cumin
- (1 tbsp, crushed) Black Pepper
- (3 tbsp) Ghost Oil [or Olive Oil]
- (4 cloves, minced) Garlic
- (1 lb) Italian Sausage
- (1 lb) Ground Beef
- (2, minced) Chocolate Habanero
- (1 cup, diced) Green Bell Pepper
- (1 minced, 1 whole) Habanero
- (4 tbsp, diced) Jalapeno
- (4 tbsp, diced) Devil's Tongue
- (3 minced, 1 whole) Ghost Chili
- (2 oz) Dark Chocolate
- (2 tsp) Kosher Salt
- (3 tbsp, chopped) Cilantro

Curried Sea Scallops & Risotto au Terre

Seared sea scallops served with an earthy, beef flavored ghost chili risotto

Preparation

Dice WHITE BUTTON MUSHROOMS.
In small saucepan over medium heat pour in BEEF STOCK.
Add GHOST CHILI and ½ of the MUSHROOMS to the BEEF STOCK.
Pat SEA SCALLOPS dry on a paper towel and sprinkle SALT, BLACK PEPPER and CURRY POWDER on each side.

Method

In large pan over medium heat melt 2 tbsp BUTTER.
Add ARBORIO RICE and sauté for 3 minutes. Pour MARSALA WINE into the rice and reduce until nearly dry. Ladle the hot BEEF STOCK into the rice. Continuously stir and cook down until the stock is absorbed. Repeat until the stock is gone (roughly 15 minutes).
Stir in PARMESAN CHEESE, remaining BUTTER and remaining MUSHROOMS. Season with SALT and BLACK PEPPER.
In pan over medium-high heat add GHOST OIL
Place SCALLOPS one at a time (largest to smallest) in pan.
Cook for 2 ½ minutes and turn SCALLOPS (smallest to largest).
Cook for 2 ½ minutes and remove from pan.
Plate the RISOTTO AU TERRE in small scallop shaped rings alternating with the SEA SCALLOPS.

Yield: Serves 2.

Ingredient List

- (10) **White Button Mushrooms**
- (32 oz) **Beef Stock**
- (3 tbsp, minced) **Ghost Chili**
- (14) **Sea Scallops**
- (1 tbsp) **Sea Salt**
- (2 tbsp) **Black Pepper**
- (1 tbsp) **Curry Powder**
- (4 tbsp) **Butter**
- (1 lb) **Arborio Rice**
- (1/4th cup) **Marsala Wine**
- (1/2 cup) **Parmesan Cheese**
- (2 tbsp) **Ghost Oil** [or Olive Oil]

A unique new twist on "Surf and Turf" – the Risotto acts as Beef, both with its flavor and al dente bite.

Habanero Pork Tenderloin with Apple Lambic Glaze

Pork tenderloin marinated and glazed with habanero and apples

Preparation

In a food processor, create marinade by combining APPLE CIDER VINEGAR, SUGAR, DRY MUSTARD, GARLIC, 1 HABANERO and KOSHER SALT.
Marinate PORK TENDERLOIN overnight.

Method

In medium saucepan over high heat, create glaze by combining APPLE LAMBIC, APPLE SAUCE, BROWN SUGAR, CINNAMON and 1 HABANERO. Whisk to incorporate and simmer to reduce by half.

Remove PORK TENDERLOIN from marinade and brush with some of the APPLE LAMBIC GLAZE. Over medium high heat, grill PORK TENDERLOIN until done, around 12 minutes (or until internal temperature is 160 degrees).

Remove PORK TENDERLOIN from grill and cover, allowing pork to rest for 5 minutes prior to slicing into medallions.

Drizzle the remaining APPLE LAMBIC GLAZE over the pork and serve with DICED APPLES on top.
Yield: Serves 4.

Ingredient List

- (1 1/2 tbsp) Apple Cider Vinegar
- (1 tbsp) Sugar
- (1/2 tsp) Dry Mustard
- (2 cloves, minced) Garlic
- (2, minced) Habanero
- (1/2 tsp) Kosher Salt
- (1 lb) Pork Tenderloin
- (3 cups) Apple Lambic
- (1 cup) Apple Sauce
- (1/2 cup) Brown Sugar
- (1 tbsp) Cinnamon
- (1, diced) Red Delicious Apple
- (1, diced) Granny Smith Apple
- (1, diced) Gala Apple

Apple Lambic is a flavored Belgian beer that imparts a subtle apple flavor along with a delicate sweetness to the pork.

Russian Roulette Poppers
A playful take on jalapeno poppers that blast your tastebuds with flavor

Preparation

Fill deep fryer with GHOST OIL and preheat to 375 degrees.
In a small pan over medium-high heat, add BACON and fry.
Drain the BACON and crumble into small pieces.
Slice PEPPERS down the middle and gently remove the seeds and membrane.

In a medium bowl, combine the CHEDDAR CHEESE, MONTERREY JACK CHEESE, BACON, SALT, PEPPER and OREGANO. Mix well.

Stuff the PEPPERS with the BACON AND CHEESE MIXTURE.

Method

In small bowl, lightly beat EGGS.
In another small bowl, add PANKO BREAD CRUMBS.
Dip PEPPERS in egg wash, coat in PANKO.
Allow PEPPERS to sit for 2 minutes.
Dip the PEPPERS in egg wash a second time and coat in PANKO again. Fry the POPPERS for 3-5 minutes or until golden brown. Drain and serve with Ranch Dipping Sauce.

Yield: Makes 6 Russian Roulette Poppers.

Ingredient List

- (for deep frying) Ghost Oil
- (6 strips) Bacon
- (1) Ghost Chili
- (1) Devil's Tongue
- (1) Chocolate Habanero
- (1) Orange Habanero
- (1) Serrano Pepper
- (1) Jalapeno
- (1/4th cup) Cheddar Cheese
- (1/4th cup) Monterrey Jack Cheese
- (1 tbsp) Oregano
- (2 tsp) Kosher Salt
- (2 tsp) Black Pepper
- (2 cups) Panko Bread Crumbs
- (3) Eggs

Using peppers of varying heat make this appetizer a fun party game.

Take turns spinning the plate and eat what lands in front of you.

Phaal

An excruciatingly delicious indian curry dish chock full of fire and spice

Preparation

Preheat oven to 350 degrees.

In a small, dry pan over medium heat, toast the CORIANDER SEEDS until fragrant (1-2 minutes).

Crush the CORIANDER SEEDS in mortar & pestle.

In a small bowl, mix the CORIANDER, CUMIN, CHILI POWDER and GARAM MASALA with WATER to form a SPICE PASTE.

Method

In a small pot over medium heat add 1 ½ tbsp of GHOST OIL. Sauté the ONION, GARLIC and GINGER until ONIONS are translucent (5 minutes). Add the GHOST CHILI and cook for 1 minute. Add the SPICE PASTE and simmer for 10 minutes, stirring often. Add TOMATO SAUCE, DICED TOMATOES and KETCHUP. Cook for 10 minutes.

In medium pan over medium-high heat, add 1 ½ tbsp of GHOST OIL. Sauté the BEEF until browned (about 5 minutes). Drain the BEEF and add to the pot with the tomato mixture. Pour the PHAAL into a large oven-proof container and cover with tin foil. Bake for 45 Minutes. Serve with Naan Bread,

Yield: Serves 4.

Ingredient List

(1 tsp) **Coriander Seeds**
(1 tsp) **Cumin**
(3 tsp) **Chili Powder**
(2 tsp) **Garam Masala**
(1 tbsp) **Water**
(3 tbsp) **Ghost Oil** [or Olive Oil]
(1, diced) **White Onion**
(10 cloves, minced) **Garlic**
(1 tsp, minced) **Ginger**
(2, minced) **Ghost Chili**
(1 tbsp) **Tomato Sauce**
(14 1/2 oz) **Diced Tomatoes**
(2 tbsp) **Ketchup**
(1 1/2 lbs, cubed) **Beef**

This "can't stop eating" dish is perfect on a cold day.

It allows you to save on heating costs as it transforms your stomach into a furnace.

Sesame Chicken

Fried chicken pieces coated in a spicy glaze and sesame and ghost chili seeds

Preparation

Deseed and mince GHOST CHILI PEPPERS, reserve and dry seeds. Dice CHICKEN BREAST into even pieces.

Create marinade by combining 2 tsp SOY SAUCE, 1 tsp SESAME OIL, FLOUR, WATER, BAKING POWDER, BAKING SODA, 2 tbsp CORNSTARCH, SHERRY and 1 GHOST CHILI. Allow CHICKEN to marinate for 30 minutes to an hour.

Method

Fill deep fryer with VEGETABLE OIL and preheat to 375 degrees. In medium pot over medium-high heat, combine CHICKEN BROTH, 1/4th cup CORNSTARCH, SUGAR, VINEGAR, GARLIC, CHILI PASTE, 3 tbsp SOY SAUCE, 1 GHOST CHILI and 2 tbsp SESAME OIL and simmer for 10 minutes, stirring occasionally until thickened.

Remove CHICKEN from marinade and carefully drop pieces into the fryer. Cook until golden brown and swimming at the top. Drain and pat CHICKEN dry. In small dry pan over high heat, toast SESAME and GHOST CHILI SEEDS for 30 seconds. Toss the CHICKEN pieces in the sauce and sprinkle seed mixture over top. Serve over rice with stir-fried vegetables.

Yield: Serves 4

Ingredient List

- (3, minced) **Ghost Chili**
- (2 lbs) **Chicken Breast**
- (2 tsp and 3 tbsp) **Soy Sauce**
- (1 tsp and 2 tbsp) **Sesame Oil**
- (2 tbsp) **Flour**
- (4 tbsp) **Water**
- (1/4th tsp) **Baking Powder**
- (1/4th tsp) **Baking Soda**
- (2 tbsp and 1/4th cup) **Cornstarch**
- (2 tbsp) **Sherry**
- (for frying) **Vegetable Oil**
- (1 cup) **Chicken Broth**
- (1 cup) **Sugar**
- (1/4th cup) **Vinegar**
- (3 cloves, minced) **Garlic**
- (2 tsp) **Chili Paste**
- (1 tbsp) **Sesame Seeds**
- (1 tbsp) **Ghost Chili Seeds**

This is not your typical American-Chinese takeout.

Chocolate Pot de Creme with Ghost Chili Candy

A decadent chocolate custard topped with sugar crusted volcanic candy

Preparation

Cut ORANGE PEELS and 2 GHOST CHILIES into thin Strips. Crush CORIANDER SEEDS. Place 3 cups of cool WATER in a pan with CORIANDER SEEDS. Add ORANGE PEELS and sliced GHOST CHILIES. Bring mixture to a boil and drain.

In a separate pot, whisk 4 ½ cups SUGAR with 4/ 1/2 cups WATER and simmer for 15 minutes. Add ORANGE PEELS and sliced GHOST CHILIES and simmer for 1 hour.. Remove from the sugar mixture and carefully drain. Lightly roll pieces in SUGAR to coat and refrigerate until needed.
Preheat oven to 325 Degrees.

Method

In small saucepan, add MILK, and whole GHOST CHILI. Heat MILK to a simmer. and remove GHOST CHILI. Add CHOCOLATE, 1 cup SUGAR and stir until incorporated. Remove from heat and add VANILLA and GRAND MARNIER. Whisk EGG YOLKS together and slowly pour into the chocolate mixture. Pour the custard into ramekins and place ramekins into an empty pot. Fill pot with water 3/4ths of the way up the ramekins. Bake for 40 minutes. Remove and refrigerate until chilled. Garnish with ORANGE PEEL AND GHOST CHILI CANDY.
Yield: Serves 6

Ingredient List

- (2) **Orange Peels**
- (16) **Coriander Seeds**
- (3 cups + 4 1/2 cups) **Water**
- (1 whole + 2 sliced) **Ghost Chili**
- (1/2 cup + 6 cups) **Sugar**
- (1 pint) **Milk**
- (8 oz) **Bittersweet Chocolate**
- (1 tsp) **Vanilla Extract**
- (1 oz) **Grand Marnier**
- (7) **Egg Yolks**

The inspiration for this dish came from drinking a refreshing orange and coriander spiced Belgian style beer.

The candy can be eaten with the dish or on its own.

Mango Lassi
A refreshing indian mango yogurt drink

Method

Add MANGO, MILK, YOGURT, SUGAR and CARDAMOM into a blender.

Blend until smooth.

Pour into glass and sprinkle CARDAMOM on top. Garnish with MINT LEAVES

Yield: Makes 2 drinks.

Ingredient List

(2, diced) **Mango**
(4 1/2 oz) **Milk**
(8 oz) **Yogurt**
(1/4th cup) **Sugar**
(1/8th tsp) **Cardamom**
(garnish) **Mint Leaves**

Congratulations. You've read, cooked and eaten your way through the hottest cookbook on the planet.

Drink this. It should do just the trick to soothe your burns.

Enjoy!

Made in the USA
Lexington, KY
12 December 2012